Son

I love you because

because

I Love You Because Books
www.riverbreezepress.com

To My Son _____

Love, _____

Date: _____

One of the best things about you is your

_____

I am amazed by your talent for

_____

I think it's awesome that you

_____

You should win the
grand prize for

_____

I am so proud of you for

_____

I love you more than

_____

I love when you tell me about

_____

I love when we

---

together

You have taught me to appreciate

_____

Thank you for being patient with me when

_____

I wish I could

---

as well as you

I love that we have the same

_____

You should be the
king of

_____

If you were a superhero you would be

_____

You make me laugh
when you

_____

I wish I had more time to

_____

with you

You make the best

_____

You have inspired me to

_____

If I could give you anything it would be

_____

I would love go

with you

I remember when we used to

_____

I love you
because you are

_____

Made in the USA
Middletown, DE
23 April 2022